Zoom

For Beginners

A Complete Beginner's Guide to Getting Started with Zoom for Webinar, Live Stream, Meeting, Video Conferencing Plus Additional Tips and Tricks for Zoom

Aaron Baddey

CONTENTS

INTRODUCTION 1
LESSON 1 2
WHAT IS ZOOM? 2
FEATURES OF ZOOM 3
ZOOM ACCOUNT TYPES 4
LESSON 2 7
GUIDE TO GETTING STARTED WITH ZOOM 7
ZOOM APP DOWNLOADS 7
ZOOM OUTLOOK PLUGIN 8
ZOOM BROWSER EXTENSIONS 8
USING ZOOM IN YOUR BROWSER 9
ZOOM FREE AND PAID USERS 9
ZOOM SET UP 11
SIGN UP AN ACCOUNT 11
ZOOM WEB PORTAL 12
ZOOM DESKTOP CLIENT 12
LESSON 3 14
ZOOM MEETINGS 14
SCHEDULING MEETINGS WITH ZOOM 14
WEB PORTAL 16
ZOOM DESKTOP CLIENT 16
OUTLOOK PLUGIN 16
AUDIO AND VIDEO CONTROL 17
VIDEO 18
INVITE 19
MANAGE PARTICIPANTS 19
SHARE SCREEN 21
ADVANCED SHARING OPTIONS 22

CHAT	22
RECORD	23
THINGS TO NOTE BEFORE THE MEETING	24
HOSTING A MEETING	24
TURN THE CAMERA ON	24
WHAT YOU NEED TO GET STARTED	25
ACCESSING ZOOM AS AN ATTENDEE	25
I AM HAVING TROUBLE JOINING A MEETING. WHAT CAN I DO?	26
LESSON 4	28
ZOOM SETTINGS	28
GENERAL	28
AUDIO SETTINGS	28
VIDEO SETTINGS	29
RECORDING	29
ADVANCED FEATURES	29
STATISTICS	30
ACCESSIBILITY	30
FEEDBACK	30
CONTACTS	30
GROUPS	31
LESSON 5	32
ZOOM TIPS AND TRICKS	32
CREATE RECURRING MEETINGS	32
HOW TO RECORD ZOOM CALLS AS A VIDEO	32
RECORDING ZOOM MEETINGS ON MOBILE	34
WHERE DOES ZOOM SAVE RECORDINGS?	35
ZOOM VIRTUAL BACKGROUNDS	35
HOW TO USE VIRTUAL BACKGROUNDS ON DESKTOP	36

HOW TO USE VIRTUAL BACKGROUNDS ON THE MOBILE APP 37
TOUCH UP MY APPEARANCE 37
RECORDING TRANSCRIPTS 38
49-PERSON GALLERY VIEW 38
ZOOM SCREEN SHARING AND USING PAUSE SHARE 39
SHARE AND ANNOTATE ON MOBILE 39
ZOOM KEYBOARD SHORTCUTS 40

Introduction

Zoom is a video conferencing and instant messaging solution available to all students, instructors, and employees. Zoom is useful for enhancing web-basedclasses because it is integrated with Blackboard. It is used for scheduled meetings as well as for impromptu meetings like virtual office hours or one-on-one and group study meetings. In addition, zoom can be used for live streams, web-based seminars, video conferencing and so on.

Zoom allows you to virtually interact with co-workers or employers when in-person meetings aren't possible. This makes telecommuting seem much more human, as it helps you feel connected. With the COVID-19 coronavirus wreaking havoc across the world, for instance, Zoom has become an essential tool for small-, medium-, and large-sized teams that want to keep in touch and continue their daily workflow with minimal disruption. This guide has been prepared to take you on a journey with the new world technology "zoom" for ease of networking with your family, friends, business partners, colleagues, and all that are concerned with web-based conferencing.

Lesson 1

What is Zoom?

Zoom is a cloud-based video conferencing service you can use to virtually meet with others - either by video or audio-only or both, all while conducting live chats - and it lets you record those sessions to view later. Over half of Fortune 500 companies reportedly used Zoom in 2019. Zoom features events like:

- Meetings
- Video webinar (Web-based seminars)
- Conference rooms
- Phone systems
- Live chats, etc.

When people are talking about Zoom, you'll usually hear the following phrases:

- Zoom Meeting
- Zoom Room
- Zoom Meeting refers to a video conferencing meeting that's hosted using Zoom. You can join these meetings via a webcam or phone. Each Zoom meeting has the following features:
- Multiple video feeds (up to 25)
- Group annotations

2

- Simultaneous screen share
- Chat
- Breakout rooms
- Whiteboards

Zoom Room is the physical hardware setup that lets companies schedule and launch their Zoom Meetings from their conference rooms.

Zoom Rooms require an additional subscription on top of a Zoom subscription and are an ideal solution for larger companies.

Features of Zoom

Below are the core features of zoom:

i. **One-on-one meetings**: Host unlimited one-on-one meetings even with the free plan.
ii. **Group video conferences**: Host up to 500 participants (if you purchase the "large meeting" add-on).

   The free plan, however, allows you to host video conferences of up to 40 minutes and up to 100 participants.

iii. **Screen sharing**: Meet one-on-one or with large

groups and share your screen with them so they can see what you see.

Zoom Account Types

Zoom allows one-to-one chat sessions that can grow into group calls, training sessions and webinars for internal and external audiences, and global video meetings with up to 1,000 participants and as many as 49 on-screen videos. The free tier allows unlimited one-on-one meetings but limits group sessions to 40 minutes and 100 participants. Paid plans start at $15 per month per host.

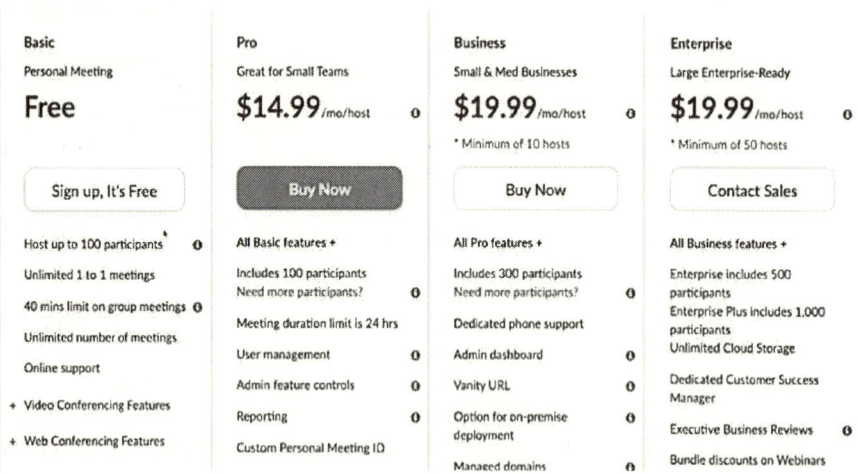

Zoom offers four pricing tiers (not including a Zoom Room subscription). Below are the basic account subscription types for zoom:

i. **Zoom Free**: This tier is free. You can hold an unlimited number of meetings. Group meetings with multiple participants are capped at 40 minutes in length, and meetings can't be recorded.
ii. **Zoom Pro**: This tier costs $14.99/£11.99 per month and meeting host. It allows hosts to create personal meeting IDs for repetitive Zoom Meetings, and it allows meeting recording in the cloud or your device, but it caps group meeting duration at 24 hours.
iii. **Zoom Business**: This tier costs $19.99/£15.99 per month and meeting host (10 minimum). It lets you brand Zoom meetings with vanity URLs and company branding, and it offers transcripts of Zoom meetings recorded in the cloud, as well as dedicated customer support.
iv. **Zoom Enterprise**: This tier costs $19.99/£15.99 per month and per meeting host (100 minimum) and is meant for businesses with 1,000+ employees. It offers unlimited cloud storage for recordings, a customer success manager, and discounts on webinars and Zoom Rooms.
v. **Optional - Zoom Rooms**: If you want to set up Zoom Rooms, you can sign up for a free 30-day trial, after which Zoom Rooms require an extra

$49/£39 per month and room subscription, while webinars using Zoom cost $40/£32 per month and host.

Lesson 2

Guide to Getting Started with Zoom

There are various ways of making use of the Zoom. It can be installed on your devices (PC or Mobile devices) and at the same time, it can be accessed directly using their web page. Below are the various means of connecting on Zoom

Zoom App Downloads

The desktop app is available for Windows and macOS, while the mobile app is available for Android and iOS. All the apps let you join a meeting without signing in, but also let you sign in using a Zoom account, Google, Facebook, or SSO. From there, you can start a meeting, join a meeting, share your screen in a Zoom Room by entering the meeting ID, start Zoom Meetings, mute/unmute your mic, start/stop the video, invite others to the meeting, change your screen name, do in-meeting chat, and start a cloud recording.

If you're a desktop user, you can also start a local recording, create polls, broadcast your Facebook live on Facebook, and more. In other words, the desktop app is more fully featured, although, if you're a free user, you can still get a lot of mileage from the mobile app.

Before you can host a meeting with Zoom, you must install the Zoom Desktop Client software for your computer/device. Start by going to https://wpi.zoom.us and select Download Client from the gray toolbar at the bottom of the login page.

Zoom Outlook Plugin

As well as the various other Zoom app downloads, it is also possible to use Zoom in other ways. For example, there's a Zoom Outlook plugin that's designed to work directly in your Microsoft Outlook client or as an Add-in for Outlook on the web. This Outlook plug drops a Zoom button right into the standard Outlook toolbar and lets you start or schedule a Zoom meeting with a simple click.

Zoom Browser Extensions

Another tool for quickly starting or scheduling a Zoom meeting comes in the form of an extension for your favorite browser. There is a Zoom Chrome extension and Zoom Firefox add-on that let you schedule a Zoom meeting via Google Calendar. A simple click on the Zoom button and you can start a meeting or schedule one for later with all the information on the meeting being sent via Google Calendar to make it easy for participants to join.

Using Zoom in Your Browser

It's fairly tricky to join a Zoom meeting in your browser without using the app. It is possible however, for example, you can join a meeting directly by using a Zoom web client link that looks something like this:

zoom.us/wc/join/your-meeting-id.

Some clever bods have also worked out a browser extension that lets you join a Zoom meeting straight from your browser without the hassle of the app. This is ideal if you're on a secure work laptop that doesn't let you install any apps for example.

This extension is currently available for Chrome and Firefox. Though it is worth noting it's not officially created by Zoom.

Zoom Free and Paid Users

Free users

You can download the Zoom app on your computer or phone and join any meeting with a supplied meeting ID. You can choose to disable audio or video before joining, too. You could even create your free Zoom account, like by linking your Google account, and from there you can create a new meeting, schedule one, join a meeting, share a screen, add contacts, and so on.

Just keep in mind you can only be signed in to Zoom on one computer, one tablet, and one phone at a time. If you sign in to an additional device while logged into another device of the same type, Zoom said you will be logged out automatically on the first device.

Paid users

You can sign up and download Zoom onto your computer using your work email if your system administrator has a Pro, Business, or Enterprise account. You'll then want to sync Zoom to your calendar so you can schedule Zoom meetings and invite remote participants to join.

If you're setting up a Zoom Room, you'll need a computer to sync and run Zoom Meetings and a tablet for attendees to launch the Zoom Meetings. You'll also need a mic, camera, and speaker, at least one HDTV monitors to display remote meeting participants, and an HDMI cable to share computer screens on a display, as well as an internet cable for your connection

You'll also need to download "Zoom Rooms for Conference Room" on the in-room computer and "Zoom Room Controller" for the tablet in the meeting room. You can then sync those rooms to your company's shared calendar so employees can see which meeting rooms are available.

Zoom Set Up

Your zoom set up can be done on two basic platforms; zoom web portal and through the desktop client software.

Sign Up an Account

You can sign up a free account with zoom by going to this web address *www.zoom.us/signup* then enter your details as required. You can also sign in by using your google, Facebook or SSO details, to do this visit: *www.zoom.us/signin.*

🔑	Sign in with SSO
G	Sign in with Google
f	Sign in with Facebook

Zoom Web Portal

Go to *https://wpi.zoom.us* and click Sign In to log in with your WPI username and password. Upon sign in you will be taken to your Profile page. Highlights of this page are:

i. Setting your avatar.
ii. Edit your Personal Meeting ID/Personal Vanity URL: This is your personal, dedicated virtual room. You can use it at any time or schedule it for future use. The meeting ID must be a 10-digit number that is also used for participants when using the telephone dial-in but the vanity URL can be set to any alpha-numeric ID (e.g. your name) that will be easy to remember.

After configuring your profile, I recommend that you go to the Meeting Settings tab to configure your preferences based on how you would like to conduct meetings.

Zoom Desktop Client

i. Once the Zoom Client for Meetings is installed, click the Sign In button
ii. Click Sign In with SSO

iii. Enter "wpi" (without the quotes) when prompted for the company domain
iv. Enter in your WPI username and password on the login screen. You now have the Zoom client for Meetings installed.

Lesson 3

Zoom Meetings

Scheduling Meetings with Zoom

You may use your Zoom user interface to schedule a meeting without logging into the Zoom website.

Set up the date, time, and duration of the meeting. Remember that the time is limited to 40 minutes for more than 2 participants for all basic accounts.

You can set a meeting to Recurring meeting if you would like the same Meeting ID number to be used for the meeting every time it is launched. This is intended for repetitive meeting.

You may restrict the video and audio options for the host (yourself) and participants of the meeting. Usually these settings can stay at the default unless you have a specific reason to change them.

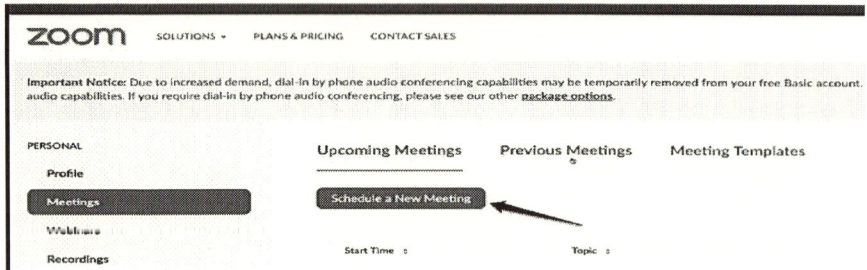

Under Meeting Options, you can require a meeting password if necessary. Expanding the Advanced Options section gives the ability to allow the participants to join before the host and start chatting via the chat window or video interface, to use your Personal meeting ID, and to record the meeting automatically on your computer. If you intend to record the meeting, please notify all participants at the start of the meeting. Once you have configured your meeting, select Schedule. The Meeting Invitation window will pop up once the meeting is scheduled in Zoom. You may use the Copy to Clipboard option to copy the invitation text to an email or calendar invitation and send to all the intended participants. If these participants have not used Zoom before, be certain to send them the Zoom meeting or user guides to help familiarize them with the software before they start.

Note that Zoom will not send you a reminder about this meeting; it must be entered into your calendar. Once created, the meeting will show on the Meetings tab of your Zoom User Panel and you may start the meeting from there using the Start button. You also have the options to Edit, Copy or Delete the meeting from this panel. Note that all participants will not be updated

15

unless you send updated information about the meeting.

Zoom offers you several ways to schedule your meetings.

Web Portal

1. Log in to https://wpi.zoom.us/
2. Click Schedule a Meeting in the top navigation bar
3. Input details for the meeting and click Save
4. You can then copy the URL or Invitation or add to your calendar with available plug in

Zoom Desktop Client

1. Click Schedule button on the Zoom App
2. Input details for the meeting and click Save
3. You can then copy the URL or Invitation or add to your calendar with available plug in

Outlook Plugin

1. Download the Zoom Outlook plugin from https://wpi.zoom.us/download
2. Create a New Meeting in Outlook
3. Click Add Zoom Meeting

4. Input Zoom Details for the meeting and click Continue
5. Update invitation details and click Send

Details on additional features for scheduled meetings can be found here:

- Alternative Host
- Scheduling Privilege
- Meet Now-vs-Schedule Meetings
- Scheduling a Zoom Meeting that Requires Registration from a Web Link

Audio and Video Control

All the required settings can be accessed here for customization, including audio and video settings. You can use the audio button to mute your feed quickly. You can also use it to change your microphone and change your output speakers.

If your signal is not ideal and you would prefer to change to dial-in audio, select Leave Computer Audio.

Clicking on Audio Options will take you to the main settings screen. The ability to test your audio and video feeds are also here if needed under the Audio and Video sections. See the Settings section for more details.

17

The video button can be used similarly to stop video, change the source and access the main settings panel as with the audio settings.

When starting/joining a meeting, you can join the audio by phone or computer.

- Choose "Join Audio by Computer" to connect your computers mic and speakers to the Zoom Meeting. You can test you Audio sources by using the "Test Computer Audio" link when joining. Choose "Phone Call" and dial the number provided. Enter in the Meeting ID and make sure to input the
"Participant ID"

Clicking on the Mic icon will let you mute and unmute your audio once connected.

Video

Access Video settings before or during a meeting by clicking on the "Settings" icon on your Zoom Desktop Application. On the Video tab you can preview and change your camera source via the down arrow. Clicking on the Video icon will let you start and stop your video feed.

Invite

During a meeting, click "Invite" to send meeting information to more participants by email, Zoom chat, phone, or room system. At any time in an unlocked meeting, you can Invite Participants to join. You may invite via their email, or from your contact list. You can also Copy the meeting URL or copy the meeting invitation by using the buttons at the bottom left.

Alternatively, give the person you are inviting the meeting ID, which is shown at the top of the Invitation panel. In the sample photos the meeting number is *309-411-140*. If you have started a meeting in your Personal Meeting Room, this will be your Personal Meeting Room Number.

Manage Participants

The Manage Participants button will bring up the participants' pane and show all participants currently in the meeting.

For yourself, you have the ability to mute and stop your video feed from this pane. You can also rename yourself for the webinar. This can be useful if you will be broadcasting with someone else at your desk to ensure everyone knows who all the participants are at the meeting.

As the meeting host, there are also controls for the other participants. This includes chatting directly, muting or stopping video for the participant, or renaming the participant.

You can also make another participant the host of the meeting. This is especially helpful if you need a longer meeting time for multiple participants. This will use the Pro license's unlimited meeting length for that meeting.

If necessary, you may also remove a participant from the meeting. The participant will receive a notice that they have been removed from the meeting.

Finally, at the bottom of the participant panel are participant actions that apply to all, including mute all and unmute all. You may also want to automatically mute participants when they enter, play an enter or exit chime or lock the meeting. Locking the meeting restricts from any more participants being able to enter the meeting.

Mute Participants on Entry

✓ Allow Participants to Unmute Themselves

✓ Allow Participants to Rename Themselves

Play Enter/Exit Chime

Lock Meeting

Share Screen

In Zoom meetings, you have the option to Share your Screen. You may choose to share your desktop or a specific application or Window that you have open. If you choose a specific application and navigate outside that application while sharing, the feed will be paused until you return to that application. If you choose to share a video from your computer, be sure to check the Share computer sound box, which ensures that the audio of the video is shared to the group. You may want to Mute all participants before sharing a video for optimal sharing.

Note that Zoom Rooms and participants using the Zoom mobile app can only share if no one else is sharing. To share screen, follow these steps:

1. Click Share Screen

2. Choose to share your; desktop, specific application, whiteboard, camera feed
3. All participants in your meeting can share their screen
4. During screen sharing you and your attendees can use the Annotation tools for drawing, pointing, highlighting, etc.

Advanced Sharing Options

There are advanced sharing options for meetings. This includes allowing one or multiple participants to share at once, restricting the sharing to the host only, or restricting when participants can share their screens

Chat

You may send a chat message to a fellow Zoom user at any time. You can also see your recent

chats and group chats in this window, as well as any recent content that has been shared with you. The chat button allows you to open the group chat in a meeting. This will be shown to the right of the video feeds. You can choose to chat to everyone or to the host only. You may use the More button to restrict the ability of meeting attendees to chat with everyone or the host only.

You may also disable chat for meetings in the web browser Zoom page. For meetings, the chat is a good way for participants to send in questions or communicate difficulties, particularly if their audio or video feeds are lagging from the overall meeting. To get started;

1. Click "Chat" to start an in-meeting message with participants in the meeting
2. The dropdown on the chat window will allow you to message Everyone, or a specific participant

Record

As a host you can record the meeting to either the Zoom cloud or your local machine.

1. Click on the "Record" icon in the toolbar
2. Choose to record to your local computer.
3. Recording will process once the meeting ends

Things to Note Before the Meeting

- Make sure to choose the correct audio and video sources
- Have the content you intend to share prepared ahead of time
- Close applications that have pop ups

Hosting A Meeting

- Mute your mic if others are presenting/speaking
- Use "Gallery View" for smaller group/team meetings
- Share your screen- Use "New Share" to seamlessly transition between shared applications.
- Use the Annotation tools to grab and direct attention

Turn The Camera On

- Put your webcam at eye level or higher – experiment for best angles
- Use the gestures and mannerisms that you would typically use in person
- Make Eye Contact - Try to look at your webcam versus the screen

What You Need to Get Started

Once you are invited for a virtual meeting, you will receive an email, containing a link to join the meeting. When it's time to join the meeting, click on the link in the email you have received.

You will need:

- An internet connected computer, laptop, or device
- Your meeting ID number/link to join the meeting
- A headset or ear buds (if you're participating with a laptop)
- A phone (if you're unable to receive audio via your computer, laptop, or device)
- A webcam (optional)

Accessing Zoom as an Attendee

To join the meeting, click the link in the email received, you will be directed to the Zoom website and from here you will need to click 'Open URL: Zoom Launcher'.

After clicking this, a pop-up box will open asking you to complete your registration.

Please enter your details in this box and ensure you use your full name so that the meeting host can identify who has joined the meeting

I am having trouble joining a meeting. What can I do?

- If you are invited to the meeting and you already have a Zoom account, you can just sign in to Zoom to join the meeting.
- If the meeting space indicates that the meeting has ended or has not started, verify the meeting time. The meeting may have been scheduled for a different time zone.
- If you are asked to sign in to your existing Zoom account and you have forgotten your password, select the "Forgot?" link and follow the instructions on the screen.
- If the meeting window isn't loading, close your browser and try to join the meeting again. Be sure to accept or approve any alerts requiring your approval to install the Zoom meeting application, and turn off any pop-up blocker that could be preventing the Zoom meeting

window from opening.

Once you have entered your details and clicked 'Join Meeting' you will be entered into the meeting successfully.

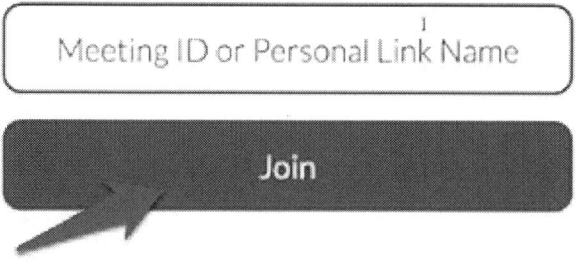

Lesson 4

Zoom Settings

The settings button in the upper left of the home screen of your Zoom user panel can be used to set up the operation of the Zoom software.

General

This tab controls items such as:

- Starting Zoom when Windows opens
- Content sharing options
- Instant messaging or chat options

Note that for all settings there are additional options that can be enabled in your account through the Zoom website.

Audio Settings

This tab contains the ability to test the computer audio and microphone, select the hardware to use for audio and microphone and determine automatic audio options.

Video Settings

The video tab allows you to select the appropriate webcam and its ratio, as well as test your video feed. You also have the ability to mirror your feed and touch up your appearance.

This tab also contains options for changing video feeds in meetings such as:

- Display participant name on video
- Turn off video when joining a meeting
- Hiding non video participants

If enabled via a web browser in your Zoom account, you will have the ability to use a virtual background for your videos. This requires a green screen for optimal performance.

Recording

The recording tab sets the default recording location, or you may select to choose the location at the end of every meeting.

Advanced Features

This tab takes you to the Zoom website.

Statistics

This shows the overall usage load on your computer and the amount attributed to Zoom. This tab should be consulted if Zoom is lagging.

Accessibility

This tab includes the option to keep meeting controls on at all time, keyboard shortcuts, and options for the size of closed captioning if enabled by the meeting host.

Note that closed captions must be typed by someone involved in the meeting and are not automatically generated.

Feedback

Use this tab to send feedback to the Zoom team. This also includes a link to the Support webpage.

Contacts

Your contacts are shown in the Contacts pane of the Zoom user panel. Here you can see the status of their contacts – whether they are online and if so, if they are online via mobile or desktop. You may select any person to either chat or meet with from this pane.

Groups

You may set up contact groups to easily access a group of contacts you would like to meet with

or chat with regularly. In that case, the group and its online members will also be shown in this pane. From here, you can chat or meet with the group.

You may send a chat message to a fellow Zoom user at any time. You can also see your recent chats and group chats in this window, as well as any recent content that has been shared with you.

Lesson 5

Zoom Tips and Tricks

Create Recurring Meetings

Zoom lets you create recurring meetings. You can set the call settings you want once and have them be in there every time you plan to meet, and you can join calls using the same URL each time. In the Zoom mobile app, just log in, click schedule, tap the Repeat option, and select a recurrence. For more info on scheduling meetings in general and all of the meeting settings, see Zoom's FAQ on scheduling meetings.

How to Record Zoom Calls as A Video

Zoom lets you record calls as videos. You do need permission to do so though. The meeting host will have to enable recordings in settings.

It's worth checking your account settings to make sure recording is enabled before you get started.

To check your account settings, follow these steps:

- Log into your zoom account
- Click to view Account Settings/Meeting settings

- Navigate to the Recording tab and click to enable video recording

It's worth noting that Zoom admins can activate recording for everyone, for users or groups.

In order to record a Zoom meeting, you must choose whether to use the local or cloud option.

Local means you store the video file yourself on your computer or in another storage area. With **Cloud**, which is for paid subscribers only, Zoom stores the video for you in its cloud storage.

But, to record videos, you need Zoom on macOS, Windows, or Linux. When you record a meeting and choose Record to the Cloud, the video, audio, and chat text is recorded in the Zoom cloud.

When the Zoom call begins you should see an option to record on the bottom of the screen. Clicking that then lets you record locally or in the cloud.

If you don't see the option to record, check your settings in the web app (under My Meeting Settings) or have your account admin enable it. The recording files can be downloaded to a computer or streamed from a browser.

During the meeting, you can also see which participants are recording the meeting and those on the meeting will also be told when the meeting is being recorded. When the call is over Zoom will automatically convert the recording into a usable MP4 video file.

Recording Zoom Meetings On Mobile

It is possible to record Zoom meetings and calls on mobile too. However, this is done via cloud recordings so you need a paid Zoom membership in order to use this feature. It's also worth noting that cloud storage is limited, so be careful how many meetings you record while using the mobile app.

To record a Zoom call on a mobile device, follow these steps:

- Open the Zoom app on your mobile
- Click to join or start a meeting
- Click the three-dot (...) menu on the bottom right of the screen
- Click "Record to the cloud" or "record"

You'll then see a recording icon and the ability to pause or stop recording

Once the call is over, you'll find the recording in the "My Recordings" section of the Zoom site

Where Does Zoom Save Recordings?

When you're recording locally, zoom call recordings are saved on the Zoom folder on your PC or Mac. These can be found at these locations:

PC: C:\Users\User Name\Documents\Zoom

Mac: /Users/User Name/Documents/Zoom

You can easily access Zoom recordings by opening the Zoom app and navigating to meetings. Once there you'll see a "recorded" tab where you can choose the meeting you need then either play the recording or open it.

For cloud storage of your Zoom meeting recordings, log in to your account and navigate to the My Recordings page.

Zoom Virtual Backgrounds

If you want to jazz things up a bit or don't want other people on the Zoom call seeing the awful mess of your home, then there's good news as Zoom offers virtual backgrounds. These are backdrops for your calls that include things like space, cityscapes and ocean-side views too.

With Zoom virtual backgrounds, you can also upload an image of anything you want to customize your background. It's available for both iPhone and desktops.

How to Use Virtual Backgrounds On Desktop

It's fairly easy to get started with Zoom virtual backgrounds. On a Mac or PC, for instance, just open up your Zoom client, click on the "Setup" icon on the corner, and select "Virtual Background" in the side menu.

Zoom provides a few virtual backgrounds. Click on the one you'd like to use. If you would like your own background, click on the plus sign above and to the left of the sample backgrounds, choose an image from your computer, and add it.

You can also add a virtual background during a meeting. In your Zoom client, click on the arrow next to the video symbol on the left, select "Choose a virtual background...", and you will see the same Virtual Background page.

The company recommends using a green screen and a good webcam to get the best results, but it is possible to use a virtual background without a green screen too.

How to Use Virtual Backgrounds On the Mobile App

You can also use Zoom virtual backgrounds on the app too. Login to your account and join a meeting via your phone. Then click the three dots at the bottom of the screen and click the "more" menu. Then click "virtual background" and choose the background you want to use.

Touch Up My Appearance

As well as virtual backgrounds, Zoom offers the ability to improve your looks when you're on a call. There's a feature called "Touch Up My Appearance" which is useful if you've not had your daily caffeine fix or are struggling with life in the home office.

Touch Up My Appearance uses a filter to subtly smooth fine lines and it's meant to look very natural. To use Touch Up My Appearance, go to Settings, and under the Video tab, check the box next to Touch up.

Recording Transcripts

As well as recording Zoom meetings, you can also automatically transcribe the audio of a meeting that you record to the cloud. And, as the meeting host, you can edit your transcript, scan the transcript text for keywords to access the video at that moment, and share the recording.

To enable the Audio Transcript feature for your own use, sign into the Zoom web portal and navigate to My Meeting Settings, then go to the Cloud recording option on the Recording tab, and verify that the setting is enabled. Choose **Turn On**, if need be. If the option is greyed out, it has been locked at either the Group or Account level, and you will need to contact your Zoom admin.

49-Person Gallery View

With gallery view, you see up to 49 meeting participants at once, rather than the default 25, depending on your device.

With the Zoom mobile app on Android and iOS, you can start or join a meeting. By default, the Zoom mobile app displays the active speaker view. If one or more participants join the meeting; you will see a video thumbnail in the bottom-right corner. You can view up to four participants' video at the same time.

If you want to view 49 people, you will need the Zoom desktop client for macOS or Windows. Once you have the desktop app installed on your computer, you must go to Settings and click Video to display the video settings page. Then, enable the option "Display up to 49 participants per screen in Gallery View".

Zoom Screen Sharing and Using Pause Share

Did you know that you can not only share your screen (smartphone and desktop) but also pause your screen sharing? Simply press Pause Share when you don't want your meeting participants to watch you mess around your presentation slides. Learn more here.

Share and Annotate On Mobile

You can share files directly from your phone while in the meeting and use the white boarding feature on your phone by writing comments with your finger. To annotate while viewing someone else's shared screen, select View Options from the top of the Zoom window, and then choose Annotate. A toolbar will appear with all your options for annotating - such as text, draw, arrow, and so on.

Zoom Keyboard Shortcuts

It's possible to use various shortcut keys during Zoom meetings to access features or change settings easily. These include a multitude of things but our favorites are:

- Alt + A or Command (⌘) +Shift+A: Mute/unmute audio
- Alt+M or Command (⌘) +Control+M: Mute/unmute audio for everyone except the host
- Alt+S or Command (⌘) +Control+S: Start screen sharing
- Alt+R or Command (⌘) +Shift+R: Start/stop local recording
- Alt+C or Command (⌘) +Shift+C: Start/stop cloud recording
- Alt+P or Command (⌘) +Shift+P: Pause or resume recording
- Alt+F1 or Command (⌘) +Shift+W: Switch to active speaker view in video meeting

Made in the USA
Coppell, TX
25 June 2020